The Courageous Chiropractor and the Night Mare

Jennie Lynn Gillham
Samantha Kingdon, DC

Illustrations by Michelle Barnett

Special thanks to the Simmons family, Gillham family,
and our wonderful editor, Lindsey Marcus

www.CourageousChiropractor.com

Freddy the Fox is also known as the Courageous Chiropractor. He calls home the tiny forest near the National Cowboy & Western Heritage Museum in Oklahoma City, USA. He loves to travel the world and help injured animals with chiropractic care.

Lizzy the lizard is Freddy's sidekick. When she's afraid you can always hear her humming or singing the Courageous Chiropractor song. She loves traveling the world, making new friends, and helping teach others about chiropractic care.

Find all 4 OWLS hidden in the book!

Freddy the Fox and his friend Lizzy the lizard were on their way to the Fall Festival in Thetford, England.

A squirrel skittered across the path and picked up an acorn.

"Beware of the Night Mare,"

said the squirrel.

Then it hurried into the forest.

Freddy and Lizzy
followed the path
into the woods.

Suddenly, out of
nowhere, a loud neighing
sound came from deep
in the forest.

"How about we hum my favorite song?" suggested Freddy.

Lizzy was halfway done with her third round of humming when she heard another neigh. "It's getting louder," she whispered.

A rustling sound came from the bushes. "That was as loud as a tap-dancing T-Rex," Lizzy said.

Suddenly, out of nowhere, a purple pony came from behind the bushes.

"Howdy," the fox said bravely. "I am Freddy, the courageous **Chiropractor.**"

"The **courageous kiwi putt putt?**" the pony asked.

"**Kai-ruh-prak-ter,**" Lizzy said slowly.

The pony repeated after Lizzy.

"Very good," said Lizzy.

"My name is Bella,"
the pony said.

"Are you the Night Mare?"
Lizzy asked.

"I don't think so," Bella said. "Although my purple coat makes it hard for others to see me at night. And I am a mare, a female horse."

"I was on my way to the Fall Festival when I had to stop. I'm not sure I will be able to deliver my treats because of my pain," Bella said.

"Can you tell us about your day?" asked Freddy.

"Once all the treats were made, I loaded them on the cart and slipped into the harness. When I began pulling the cart, my neck and shoulders hurt," Bella said.

"You might have a **subluxation** in your spine," Freddy said.

"A submarine named Jason?" the pony asked.

"Sub-luck-say-shun," Lizzy said.

Bella repeated after Lizzy.

"Very good," said Lizzy.

"A subluxation is when the bones are stuck in the wrong position or they are not moving well. It can come from an injury or from things you do every day. That can make it hard for you to move and can cause pain."

"I use my hands to help. I also have a tool I can use," said Freddy.
"It's called my magical mover."

Bella let out a fearful neigh.

"It's okay," Lizzy said.
She drew on the ground using her tail.

"That's a picture of me," Bella said cheerfully.

"I reckon your pain here is caused by using the cart harness day after day," Freddy said.

"Okay, I will give it a try," Bella said.

Freddy walked toward
Bella and began to
remove the harness.

Then he worked on the
base of Bella's neck.

After a minute, he pulled out his magical mover. "To make the magical mover work, you have to whistle," Freddy said, then whistled.

The magical mover went clickety-clack as it pressed down.

CLICK!

"That didn't hurt at all!" Bella said.

"How do you feel now?"
asked Lizzy.

"I feel better," Bella said.
"Thank you!"

Freddy loosened the harness,
then hooked Bella back up.

Just then, the leaves began to rustle. "Oh no. This time it really is the Night Mare!" Lizzy shouted.

Suddenly, out of nowhere, the squirrel from earlier jumped onto a nearby branch. "Howdy, friend," Freddy said.

"I don't think I can make it to the fall festival. My bag of acorns is too heavy," the squirrel said.

"You can load it onto my cart," Bella suggested.

The squirrel didn't move from his spot.

"All three of you are welcome to get a ride as well now that I feel better," Bella said.

"There's plenty of room for everyone, the bag of acorns, and my cart full of acorn-flavored muffins."

"Acorn muffins?" Lizzy asked. "That's as uncommon as a starfish shaped like a square."

"When we get to town, the three of you can hand out all the muffins with acorns on top," Bella said.

"I'm going to tell everyone about how Freddy helped me feel better and how I made new friends, too."

Suddenly, out of nowhere,
she stopped.
"What if the pain comes back after
you leave?" Bella asked.

"Just sing the courageous chiropractor song,
and I will return," said Freddy.

"I will sing it for you, but I haven't figured out
the last lines yet," Lizzy said.
As Bella trotted along the path, Lizzy began to sing...

WHEREVER THE TUMBLEWEED ROLLS

THE COURAGEOUS CHIROPRACTOR STROLLS

WHETHER DAY OR NIGHT

DARK OR LIGHT

RAIN OR SNOW

HIGH OR LOW

NEAR OR FAR

WHEREVER YOU ARE

Bella began to sing after Lizzy stopped.

OVER ROLLING WAVES OF GRASS

HE HEARD MY NEIGH

THE COURAGEOUS CHIROPRACTOR

SAVED THE DAY!

They all cheered.
Then they sang the song
again and again until
they arrived at the
Fall Festival.

Once there, Freddy, Lizzy, and the squirrel passed out all the acorn-flavored muffins with acorns on top. Bella taught everyone the courageous chiropractor song.

Freddy and Lizzy made many new friends and promised to return to the fall festival each year.

Sign up for The Courageous Chiropractor email list. You'll get:

2 Activity Pages and a Brochure
A new activity page each month
Information about upcoming books,
contests and more!

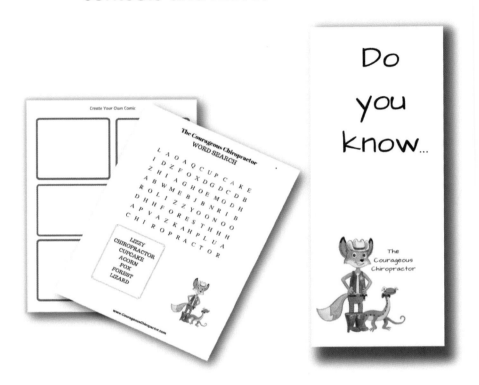

Perfect for the home or office waiting room.

Have a grown-up go to
www.CourageousChiropractor.com

Thank you for reading
The Courageous Chiropractor and the Night Mare.
Would you show your support and help us spread the word by
writing a quick book review wherever you purchased your copy?
(or you can post one at Goodreads)

Printed in Great Britain
by Amazon